THE BIGGER PICTURE

THE BIGGER PICTURE

A GUIDE TO PERSONAL, RELATIONAL, & EMOTIONAL GROWTH

KAM PHILLIPS

The Bigger Picture © Copyright 2021 by Kameron Phillips

For more information, email booking@kameronphillips.com.

ISBN: 978-1-7373916-0-9 *Paperback*
ISBN: 978-1-7373916-1-6 *E-book*

GET YOUR FREE VIRTUAL WORKBOOK

To receive free, printable worksheets listed in the book, visit:
www.kameronphillips.com/thebiggerpicture

@itskamphillips
To stay connected, feel free to hit me up on most social media platforms
Or, to subscribe to my mailing list, please visit
www.kameronphillips.com

Dedication

This book is dedicated to my Aunt Sandra. I love and miss you. You embodied love in every room you walked into and inspired me in more ways than I ever got to tell you. See you soon.

CONTENTS

INTRODUCTION

This book was created to help students and young adults discover practical ways to establish foundational character development principles and provide perspective on using those tools in various areas of life. Throughout the pages, I'll share relatable stories and interactive exercises so you can establish a solid foundation while you evolve into the best version of yourself.

Throughout my journey I've battled with low motivation, bad grades, legal trouble, complicated family relationships, lack of confidence, depression, and other mental health challenges. Once I reevaluated my lifestyle and my actions, started keeping myself accountable and listening to people who had my well-being in mind, my perspective shifted and started to elevate. I experienced things I never would have thought. I got to play ball in college, travel the world, graduate on time, get a dope job right out of school, and make a six-figure salary in my 20's.

I care about you because I know how it feels to be lost. I know how it feels to want to provide for yourself, future family, and have a successful life, but not even knowing where to start. It's tough trying to navigate through life without having much guidance. My goal has always been to inspire people to pursue opportunities they don't see as attainable. This book serves as the spark to achieve the mindset shift required to break through your self-imposed limitations.

They say that, "A smart man learns from his mistakes, but a wise man learns from others." Someone's grandma might say, "You're gonna learn the easy way or the hard way." I don't want to flex like I have all the answers, because I don't. However, I have learned a lot from my past experiences, failures, and people who are a lot more successful and smarter than I am. Honestly, you'll have to discover most of your own answers since you know your situation better than anyone. But you have to make sure you ask the right questions to get the right answers.

I want to share those essential questions and lessons that I had to learn the hard way. The quicker we invest in taking time to discover answers to the difficult questions, the easier it is to navigate our journey towards the life we envision.

Hope this book is helpful to your growth. Much love on the journey.

Free Game

I'll throw in some random "free game" throughout the book. It could be a personal mantra, quote from someone I admire, words of encouragement, or something I think adds value.

"It's the things you learn after you know it all that count." Coach John Wooden - Led UCLA to 10 NCAA Basketball Championships

Promise To Yourself

Fear is often rooted in the unknown. Fear is a complicated, sneaky, scary, and powerful emotion. *Fear can either paralyze or elevate you.* It's your choice.

The choice to try something new, re-evaluate what we think we know, and dig deep by asking ourselves the hard questions can be scary. It can be scary for our pride to admit we don't understand something. It can be scary for our ego to ask a question we don't know the answer to. **It gets even scarier if we don't like the answers we discover.**

The only way we're able to conquer fear is by focusing on something even more powerful... Love. *Personal development is about loving yourself enough to get out of your comfort zone, stretch yourself, and push yourself to grow.*

I'll leave you with this... **Do it for yourself.** If you've read this far, I know you care about elevating to the next level. Now it's time to put in the effort. If someone has to convince you, maybe you're ok with being average. But if you want to continue to level up in life, you have to invest in yourself. **Love yourself enough to spend time improving that relationship.**

I'm proud you're taking this step! But it's not about me, it's about you.

I,_____, promise to make moves out of love, not fear. I'm dedicated to invest in myself to improve my mindset, character, and future lifestyle.

Signature: _____ Date:_____

LEVEL 1

VALUES TO VISION

PERSONAL DISCOVERY STARTS BY CREATING SELF-AWARENESS THROUGH REFLECTION. ONCE WE ESTABLISH A MORAL CODE TO GUIDE OUR DECISION MAKING, IT SPURS INTERNAL MOTIVATION AND PROVIDES THE GUIDE RAILS TO REACHING OUR GOALS.

CHAPTER 1
CORE VALUES

When I was in high school, my basketball team was playing in our county's regional tournament. The way this tournament was set up, about 25 different teams would all travel to one school and play games back-to-back-to-back.

15 minutes before our game started, most of my teammates and I were in the locker room listening to music. You know, getting hype! We had a great season so far and were one of the favorites in the tournament. Our coaches left us to enjoy ourselves in the locker room and walked out to watch the other games. A few moments later, one of the younger dudes on the team walked in and turned the music down.

"Ay, the locker room next door is unlocked…"

We knew the deal. The team who was playing on the court now had left their stuff. Wallets, iPhones, headphones. Everyone started looking at each other like - *Yo, they slipped up and we're about to come up.*

About half of my teammates ended up going in and racking up – they took anything they could find. The other half ended up just walking out and pretending like they didn't hear or see anything. Fortunately, that day, I was in the other half.

We played the first half of the game and were just winning by a few points. When we walked into our locker room at halftime, two cops were waiting for us. They told us they had cameras in the hallways and my teammates got arrested on the spot.

Even though I tried to tell myself, "If I didn't steal anything, then I wasn't doing anything wrong", I knew me not speaking up and checking my homies when they were doing wrong was just as bad. I also knew I had done the same thing other times, and just never got caught.

Integrity can be defined as doing the right thing when nobody's looking. If you would have asked me back then, I would have said integrity is something that I value. But in reality, if I don't practice it, can I really claim it as important?

If we don't practice our values with the small things, we won't be prepared to stick to them when we face the hard things. It's almost impossible to stick to a value when we haven't taken the time to identify which ones are important to us.

One of the hardest questions I've been asked is...**"Who are you?"**

It's not what city you live in, the sport you play, your job title, or the grades you get...but it's the person you know you are no matter what environment you're in. This is a surprisingly tricky question if you haven't thought about it before.

If you transferred to a different school tomorrow, who would you be?

If you got injured and couldn't play the sport you're so good at, who would you be?

If you got laid off or your business shut down, who would you be?

If you moved to a different country and didn't speak their language, who would you be?

There's nothing wrong with being proud of your city, sport, or school, but all of that could change in an instant. Who you are is based on what you value and the actions you take to live by those values.

Free Game
The source of real confidence is self love & self empowerment, not validation from others

Why is it important to know your values?

A value is something that is important to us. A core value is something that's so important, we feel bad if we or our close friends don't practice it.

Values Dictate Decisions

Decisions are based on what we value the most. If we make decisions that are in line with our values, as opposed to our temporary feelings on the situation, we're happier in the long-term.

Decisions Form Your Process

Our process is created by the decisions we make on a daily basis. All of our decisions, big or little, good or bad, work together to form habits and direct our steps.

Process Guides Your Journey

Our journey is the path we take to get to a destination. Some routes are smooth when we follow our map. And some routes leave us lost because we didn't let the map guide our directions.

Journey Leads To Your Vision

Our imagination and exposure give us the ability to create a vision for our lives. How the vision turns out depends on our decisions, process, and the journey we take. It's connected.

Discover Your Core Values

To get a better feel about what's important to you, LIST THE TOP 10 values that resonate with you the most on the next page.

Values	Definition/Description
Accomplishment	To do or carry out successfully; achieving
Authenticity	Real, genuine, or true; being really what it seems to be
Balance	Mental/emotional steadiness; priorities match scheduling
Boldness	Going forward in the face of danger; bravery, courage
Compassion	Sympathy towards the struggle of others; empathy
Competitiveness	Desire to perform better than others; wanting a challenge
Creativity	Creating new things, showcasing imagination; innovation
Curiosity	Desire to learn and gain new experiences
Determination	Dedicated to getting a task done; doing whatever it takes
Fairness	Equal judgement and considering all sides; unbiased
Faith	Belief or trust without needing proof
Fun	Amusement, enjoyment, pleasure
Health	Taking care of the body and mind
Honesty	Telling the truth, not misleading others
Humor	Highlighting the amusing or funny side/perspective
Independence	Not being controlled or needing support; self-sufficient
Influence	Affecting other's actions; persuasion
Integrity	Strength of character and morals, even when alone.
Intelligence	Gaining and displaying knowledge; awareness
Joy	To be glad; feeling happy about a situation
Kindness	Being nice to others; generous or willing to share
Loyalty	Committed and dedicated to a person or goal
Optimism	Expecting the best out of everything; positivity
Peace	Free from stress or conflict
Popularity	Being liked by people; fame
Power	Control other's actions; authority
Recognition	Special attention; positive notice or status
Respect	Valuing people and opinions
Responsibility	Taking care of your part of a job; dependable, maturity
Security	Feeling safe or stable: physically, financially, or emotionally
Service	Helping and/or teaching others
Spirituality	Belief in a higher purpose or power
Unity	Coming together as one; harmony
Wisdom	Putting to use experiences or insight

Discover Your Core Values

TOP 10

_____

_____

_____

_____

_____

_____

_____

_____

_____

Once you're done with the list, TAKE A BREAK!

Discover Your Core Values

Ready? Look back at your list of 10 and SELECT THE TOP 5.
Take your time.

TOP 5

_____

_____

_____

_____

_____

Take another break.
Don't rush into the next part. Get your mind right and reset.

Discover Your Core Values

You guessed it. Look back at your list of 5 then SELECT YOUR TOP 3 core values. I know all of them are important. What represents you the most? If two of them are similar, decide on the best fit.

TOP 3

_____

_____

_____

CONGRATS!
Most people don't know what they stand for, but now you do.
KEEP LEVELING UP!

Check Your Alignment

Now, let's see how aligned you are with the core values you listed. Get your phone out, and put on a 15-minute timer. That's how long you have to complete this section.

Instructions

1. Answer all 10 questions for each of your top 3 values.
2. Measure up how aligned you are with those values.
   a. Rate each question on a scale of 1-10. 10 being the highest (No doubt!) and 1 being the lowest (Nah).
3. Add up the total scores for each value separately.
4. Review the ranking of the scores.

Example:

My favorite TV or movie character shows this value.

Value #1   1   2   3   4   5   6   (7)   8   9   10

Value #2   1   2   3   (4)   5   6   7   8   9   10

Value #3   1   2   3   4   5   6   7   8   (9)   10

Ready, Set, START!

Check Your Alignment

List your 3 core values. Order doesn't matter.

Value #1   Value #2   Value #3

_____   _____   _____

1. Most of the people I admire seem to have this value.

Value #1   1   2   3   4   5   6   7   8   9   10

Value #2   1   2   3   4   5   6   7   8   9   10

Value #3   1   2   3   4   5   6   7   8   9   10

2. If people didn't want me to support this value, I'd ignore them.

Value #1   1   2   3   4   5   6   7   8   9   10

Value #2   1   2   3   4   5   6   7   8   9   10

Value #3   1   2   3   4   5   6   7   8   9   10

3. I'm excited when people compliment me for showing this value.

Value #1   1   2   3   4   5   6   7   8   9   10

Value #2   1   2   3   4   5   6   7   8   9   10

Value #3   1   2   3   4   5   6   7   8   9   10

Check Your Alignment

4. I couldn't work well in a group with people who didn't recognize the importance of this value.

Value #1   1   2   3   4   5   6   7   8   9   10

Value #2   1   2   3   4   5   6   7   8   9   10

Value #3   1   2   3   4   5   6   7   8   9   10

5. If I were going to make a list of the perfect characteristics of a friend, this value would be one of the first things I'd put on the list.

Value #1   1   2   3   4   5   6   7   8   9   10

Value #2   1   2   3   4   5   6   7   8   9   10

Value #3   1   2   3   4   5   6   7   8   9   10

6. If there was a time I didn't stand up for this value, I'd regret it.

Value #1   1   2   3   4   5   6   7   8   9   10

Value #2   1   2   3   4   5   6   7   8   9   10

Value #3   1   2   3   4   5   6   7   8   9   10

Check Your Alignment

7. The best decisions I've made for myself supported this value.

Value #1   1   2   3   4   5   6   7   8   9   10

Value #2   1   2   3   4   5   6   7   8   9   10

Value #3   1   2   3   4   5   6   7   8   9   10

8. The worst decisions I have made for myself broke this value.

Value #1   1   2   3   4   5   6   7   8   9   10

Value #2   1   2   3   4   5   6   7   8   9   10

Value #3   1   2   3   4   5   6   7   8   9   10

9. The most memorable argument I've ever had was about this value.

Value #1   1   2   3   4   5   6   7   8   9   10

Value #2   1   2   3   4   5   6   7   8   9   10

Value #3   1   2   3   4   5   6   7   8   9   10

Check Your Alignment

10. I couldn't be in a close friendship with someone who did not share this value.

Value #1   1   2   3   4   5   6   7   8   9   10

Value #2   1   2   3   4   5   6   7   8   9   10

Value #3   1   2   3   4   5   6   7   8   9   10

Add up the total score for each value.

Value #1   Value #2   Value #3

_____   _____   _____

Check Your Alignment

What each score means:

This value is part of your code. Continue to dive into the next step to see how it shows up in your life and continues to evolve.

This value is definitely important, but might not be a non-negotiable. Take a look at those top 5 values and reflect on if recent events swayed your decision at all. Other values may rise above them during important or stressful situations.

Other values are more important than this one. Double check your list and take some time to re-read definitions. It might be important, it's just not one we shape our life around.

Stop flexing. Don't worry about what people will think and focus on the values important to YOU. All of the values have different levels of importance to everyone, so there's no "wrong" answer.

That's it! If someone asks "Who are you?", now you can let them know the type of person you are and what you stand on.

Reflection Questions

What values does my family have that make me feel safe and loved?

Do my values differ from my parents? If so, how?

Reflection Questions

Have my values ever been challenged or threatened? How did I react?

What choices can I make to protect my values?

CHAPTER 2

YOUR STORY

When I was in 5th grade, I remember having a conversation with my pops. He told me that I was gifted at getting along with different types of people and that it would help me in the future. It was one of those moments I really took to heart. At that point, I started to consciously hang with people different from me so I could learn more about them, their background, and their story.

By hearing the stories of different people, I learned that everyone has something in common. Everyone has highs and lows in life, which creates a story that's unique to them.

Personally, I've experienced a lot of highs and lows throughout life. I was taken advantage of sexually at a young age and loved dearly by my parents. I dealt with my parent's separation in middle school and met some of my best friends the same year. I saw friends get kicked out of school or go to jail and I got to graduate and play college basketball. I've been to 14 countries and been arrested 7 times. I've mourned the death of close ones and have been reborn through baptism. I've been in love four times and had my heart broken once. I've stayed in mental hospitals and penthouse suites. I've been suicidal and have shed tears of joy.

Regardless of the highs and lows you've been through and will continue to go through, keeping perspective in those situations will help you push forward. All of those experiences can help us grow if we take the time to reflect on how they fit in our bigger picture. Reflecting on your story not only has the ability to encourage you by reminding you of everything you've already conquered, but prepares you to uplift others who can relate to your past.

Why is your story important?

It's hard to know where you're going if you don't know where you've been. When we take the time to lay out our story:

1. **We gain an understanding of what's been important to us in the past.** Looking back, we can notice recurring themes and see how situations during that time affected how we felt and responded.

2. **We confirm how much we've grown over time.** It's tough to see how much we're improving in the moment and can be frustrating if we don't think we're moving fast enough. When we look at our story, it gives us a chance to reflect on our growth and encourages us to continue to grow...even if it's not obvious to us in the moment.

3. **We see what we can work on.** Have you ever looked back on a time where things might have not been going great, but you can't remember why? Reflecting on our story helps us figure out what areas we can make adjustments in so we can have a better future.

4. **We learn what makes us unique!** You're the only one who has lived your story. Point blank. Knowing what you've been through, how you've handled situations, and your motives behind your actions help you differentiate yourself from others.

Free Game
Everyone has a story. Share yours. It makes you powerful!

Journey Graph

Let's look at your story so far. The vertical is marked from +10 to -10. On the horizontal axis, you can write in either your grade or age range. On the last dash on the right side, write in your current grade or age. Then for each dash to the left, you can either mark every other dash with your previous grade *or* evenly distribute your previous years of age.

<u>For each grade or age, put a dot on how you would rank that year.</u> You can put 2 separate dots for the beginning and the middle of the year if you need. For example, if the beginning of 6th grade wasn't good, you can put a -5. If it got better in the second half, you could put another dot at +6.

Once you're done, connect the dots going from the earliest grade or year to the most recent.

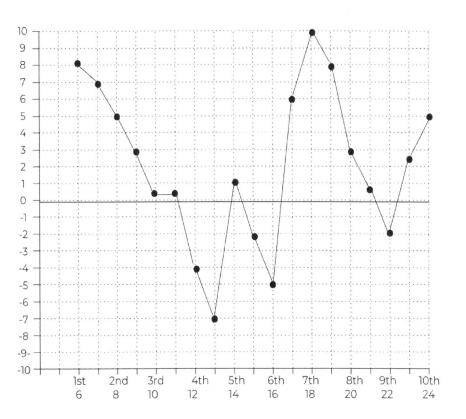

Journey Graph

Tip: Don't feel pressed to go in order. You can start by graphing your highest and lowest moments in life, then fill in the rest. This way, you have a measuring stick to compare the other years.

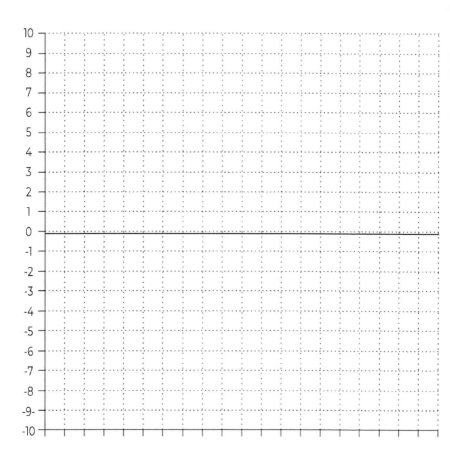

Free Game

In life you can't connect the dots going forward. You always have to connect them going back for it to make sense.

Reflection Questions

In what moments throughout your life did you feel most energized or in your flow? Who was around you? What was going on with your family, friends, school, or other activities?

What changes occurred to switch a bad year to a good year, or the opposite? Did something in your circumstances change, did your mindset change, or both? How did either change?

Reflection Questions

What 3 accomplishments are you most proud of from your past? Why are those moments important to you?

What are 2 things you're looking forward to accomplishing in the next couple of years? How do you think they will compare to a moment from the past?

CHAPTER 3

FUTURE SELF

My pops dragged me to this event when I was a teenager. It was a Saturday morning so I just wanted to sleep in, but obviously I didn't have a say in the matter. We got to this building in downtown Atlanta and waited in this cold room with a few other kids and their parents. I think they didn't want to be there just as much as me.

The program was called "Leaders of Tomorrow" and it was their career day. The only career I ever said I wanted was to play in the NBA or travel the world as a taste tester (it's lowkey still my dream job). After the program director did a brief introduction, a stylish, young Black dude walked to the front. He was a music manager. He told us his story about throwing parties in high school, learning to monetize it when he got to college, building his network, then people approaching him asking to help get the word out about their music. When he was in college, he decided to major in marketing to perfect his craft and worked with a major record label company. He got the chance to travel, work with successful musicians, and make good money.

Up to this point, college didn't really appeal to me. It just seemed like something I was expected to do. My only priority was figuring out whether I'd be able to play basketball in college, but this speaker changed my perspective because he was relatable. Most of the people I saw who had good careers either didn't look like me or I thought they were corny. By meeting someone who I could connect with, I began to imagine different alternatives for my future.

Where do you see yourself in 5 years? 10 years?

I used to hate this question. Now, I realize how important it is to explore. You don't get what you want, you get what you picture. And if you don't have a picture, you don't have expectations for yourself.

So, let me reframe the question.

Who do you expect to be in 5 years?

Who would you be proud to be in 10 years?

Who would you be disappointed to be in 7 years?

You can't be what you don't see.

In this section, we'll start to explore creating a vision. You might come across some questions you've never thought about or don't immediately know the answer to, and that's cool! It's all about growth and that requires doing things we haven't done.

Free Game
"Always felt like my vision been bigger than the bigger picture."
Drake - Grammy-Award winning rapper

Role Models

Let's start by looking at some other people. For the record - there's only one YOU. Don't get it twisted. That being said, everyone learns from somebody. Never let ego hold you back from learning from others.

List 3 - 5 people you admire, respect, or are in your ideal situation.

_____

_____

_____

_____

_____

Note: It can be a friend, parent, teacher, coach, or someone else in your circle. It can also be someone you don't personally know. A famous person (dead or alive), someone you follow on Instagram, or anyone you'd like to meet.

It's hard to be what you can't see. Hopefully you were able to find examples of characteristics and accomplishments that you aspire to reach in the future. If you couldn't think of anyone, keep looking! With Instagram, TikTok, YouTube, and Google, we can find examples of people doing extraordinary things without having to personally know them. If you don't think you can improve in anyway, or think you have accomplished everything you want...I'm not buying it. I have a feeling if you made it this far in the book, you're committed to still growing.

Now instead of looking at others accomplishments, characteristics, and habits...we're going to look in the mirror and in the future. This is a lot harder. You'll need your imagination. If you can't answer all of the questions in one try, that's cool. Take your time, but push yourself to keep dreaming and creating a picture for your future.

Reflection Questions

For the first 3 questions, refer to the people you listed.

What characteristics do they have that you appreciate?

What habits do they have that contributed to their success?

Reflection Questions

What would you want to learn from them?

Who are you in the future? How do you walk, talk, act, dress, who do you hang out with? Use your imagination and let it flow. Be as specific as possible.

Reflection Questions

What 24 milestones do you want to achieve in the next 5 years? Go for it! Don't be afraid to write it down.

mak more than an il	have a good shoe go
in the nfl	live life
doing what i love	get taller
have a familiy	own a bisgapa
have kids	make any own foot ball
have a cul	have my own foot ball team
have a good life	make some good mvc
not to cut my hair	have my on closes
making bans	move out
shuw love	have a billion
gave back	do all i want
be out of a gang	make my life fun

Reflection Questions

How does reaching those goals improve your situation?

If you mentioned money in these exercises - How do you want to make and sustain your money? (Keep in mind - Money is a TOOL to reach a GOAL.)

CHAPTER 4

MISSION STATEMENT

As I got older, the recurring motivation that crossed my mind was "I just have to hold it down for everyone I'm representing."

I switched up my work ethic, stayed up late grinding, and did whatever it took to stand out in order to get opportunities. People would give me compliments on different things I accomplished, whether it was passing a test or getting a promotion. After getting raise after raise and moving to higher paying roles at different companies, I still didn't feel happy. I felt like something was missing. After a big accomplishment, I would have a moment of joy then that sensation would immediately leave and emptiness would come back. I always felt like I hadn't done "enough".

One day at work, a colleague mentioned the term "impact investing". When I looked into it, I saw that it was a way to invest money while focusing on making a positive impact. I instantly got excited. I realized that my whole career I was just pursuing making money for my own benefit without realizing there were ways to both make money and serve others. My thought process to "hold it down for everyone I was representing", turned out to be me really just looking out for my own benefit and wanting to gain approval from other people. My everyday drive turned into empty actions since my accomplishments didn't serve a larger purpose. I was battling every day to push myself, but didn't even have a meaningful mission to focus on. Creating a personal mission statement helped me align my every day actions to my bigger picture goals and values.

What is a mission statement?

A mission statement guides your decision-making and how you live by your code. Earlier we broke down your core values. The personal mission is how you apply those values to impact others in your life.

Why is creating a personal mission statement important?

Your personal mission statement ties together your values and your story. It clarifies how you will stay focused and move forward towards your purpose.

How to write a personal mission statement?

The simplest way to think about it is:

Verb + Target + Result = Personal Mission

Verb: This is the thing you want to do or action you want to take.

Target: This is the group you want to help.

Result: The impact that you want to leave on that group.

Mission Statements from Public Figures

J Cole - Motivate kids to dream, believe, and achieve.

LeBron James - Positively affect the lives of children and young adults through education and co-curricular educational initiatives.

Lizzo - Put women of color, natural girls, and all kinds of black girls and big girls on a platform.

Next, we'll work on clarifying each of these areas so you can write your own personal mission statement.

Developing Your Personal Mission Statement

Let's start with remembering what's most important to us.

Value #1   Value #2   Value #3

_____   _____   _____

What breaks your heart the most when you see it?

What action(s) can be taken to help fix that issue?

Write a list of verbs that reflect an action you think you can take to help the cause.

Developing Your Personal Mission Statement

Now, let's focus on finding a group that we want to target.

What group of people experience the issues you listed? Feel free to list background, age, location, or anything that comes to mind.

Who do you find yourself connecting with the most? What group gets you energized at the thought of helping?

Developing Your Personal Mission Statement

List a few characteristics that those groups have in common.

In 4 words or less, what title or category would you give the groups based on what they have in common?

Developing Your Personal Mission Statement

Before you move on, it might be good to mention that personal mission statements are most beneficial when they are less than 20 words. You want them to be *simple and clear*. That way, you can easily point out what you're trying to do and share it with others.

Last part of the equation - The Result.

For the groups you listed, what is a possible outcome that would help solve their issue?

How can YOU help with one step to reach that outcome? What special impact can you have on the process?

Free Game:
Mission statements are going to continually evolve. As you have new experiences, feel free to comeback and build on what you wrote.

Developing Your Personal Mission Statement

Ready to put it all together? **Let's get it!**

Remember: **Verb + Target + Result = Personal Mission**

Try writing a few statements that feel right. To be honest, it's tough to figure out a mission statement on the first try. Write a few drafts and as you continue to learn more about yourself, you can settle on one strong, clear statement.

Personal Mission Statement – Draft #1

Personal Mission Statement – Draft #2

Personal Mission Statement – Draft #3

CHAPTER 5

PURPOSE DRIVEN GOALS

When I was younger, I just wanted to win. I know that sounds vague, because "just wanting to win" is vague. My competitive nature left me constantly comparing myself to other people. In order to win, I felt like I had to outshine other people. Whether it was looking better than them on the basketball court or looking cooler than them because I had more money, clothes, or girls. My goal of winning had nothing to do with succeeding in areas I personally valued, but to look like I was winning in areas the culture valued.

One day I was posed the question, "What's more important – What you acquired or who you become?" What we acquire can be seen by people on the outside, but who we become can be felt by us on the inside.

During different points in my life, I would work extremely hard so I could look like I was winning on the outside. In reality, I was just comparing my external lifestyle with other people's material things. I would pay attention to the job position my peers got or new outfits people posted on Instagram. Rarely did I take time to evaluate what would make me happy if nobody was looking. Success to me was to look like I was winning to the crowd, but I didn't actually know what winning meant – I didn't even have a game plan to win.

What is success?

Everyone wants to be happy and successful. However, *people define happiness or success in different ways*. Even though the circumstance for each person might be different, having a sense of balance in different areas of life contributes to how happy and successful you feel.

What does balance mean?

Balance is when you feel that all the areas of your life are at their full potential. *Finding balance is a constant activity, not an end goal.* There will always be areas that can be improved or areas that you're meant to focus on during a specific point of your life. The trick is being aware of how much work we need in certain areas and creating a plan on how to improve that area.

What is a purpose-driven goal?

A purpose-driven goal is when we want to achieve something for inner-motivation, not because of what other people will think. *The goal ties into what is important to us and isn't compared to other people's accomplishments.* It gets us closer to being happy, finding balance, and being successful.

Next, we'll work on identifying the gaps—areas where we can improve in different parts of our life. Then, we'll create a plan on how to level up in those areas.

Sounds good?

Grade Your Goals

Please read through the instructions for the next exercise.

1. For each light gray section, list the score you would give that area (0-100). If a section is unable to be completed, list "N/A" under that section. (Ex. An only child would list "N/A" under "Siblings")*

2. In the "GRADE & AVG SCORE" column, list the average score for the respective subject in the black bordered box. Average score = (Sum of the completed sections) divided by (total number of sections completed for that subject).

Example (Yep, more math):
- o Best Friend = 92
- o Classmates = 84
- o Extended Family = 76
- o Total = 262. Average Score = 252 / 3 = 84

3. Once the average score is listed, write down the corresponding letter grade in the dark gray box. The grading scale is listed on the sheet below.
    Example:
    - o If the average score for "Friends" is an 84, the corresponding letter grade is a "B".

FRIENDS	Best Friend	Classmates	Ext. Family (cousins, etc.)	B
List score for each section	92	84	76	84

4. Once all the subjects are completed, list the overall average score. Please use the same formula shown in #2.

5. Once the average is listed, please list the corresponding overall letter grade.

*For non-traditional families, please feel free to adapt for your discretion or use sections to reflect on your satisfaction with the living situation. *Ex: If someone does not live with their biological father or step-father, they could list score based on their relationship with a male mentor or their desire to have one.*

Grade Your Goals

From the "Journey Graph" in the Your Story section, complete the report card for the age or grade of the HIGHEST point on the graph.

Age or Grade: _____ Year: _____

SUBJECT	1ST SECTION	2ND SECTION	3RD SECTION	GRADE & AVG SCORE
FAMILY	Mother	Father	Siblings	
List score for each section				[ ]
FRIENDS	Best Friend	Classmates / Coworkers	Ext. Family (cousins, etc.)	
List score for each section				[ ]
ACTIVITIES	Hobbies	Clubs / Teams	Passion	
List score for each section				[ ]
HEALTH	Emotional / Mental	Physical	Future / Motivation	
List score for each section				[ ]
SCHOOL or WORK	Grades / Reviews	Teachers / Managers	Discipline	
List score for each section				[ ]

GRADING SCALE

A: 90-100   D: 70-73
B: 80-89   F: 0-69
C: 74-79   N/A: Not Applicable

OVERALL AVERAGE: [ ]

OVERALL GRADE: [ ]

Grade Your Goals

From the "Journey Graph" in the Your Story section, complete the report card for the age or grade of the LOWEST point on the graph.

Age or Grade: _____ Year: _____

SUBJECT	1ST SECTION	2ND SECTION	3RD SECTION	GRADE & AVG SCORE
FAMILY	Mother	Father	Siblings	
List score for each section				
FRIENDS	Best Friend	Classmates / Coworkers	Ext. Family (cousins, etc.)	
List score for each section				
ACTIVITIES	Hobbies	Clubs / Teams	Passion	
List score for each section				
HEALTH	Emotional / Mental	Physical	Future / Motivation	
List score for each section				
SCHOOL or WORK	Grades / Reviews	Teachers / Managers	Discipline	
List score for each section				

GRADING SCALE

A: 90-100   D: 70-73
B: 80-89   F: 0-69
C: 74-79   N/A: Not Applicable

OVERALL AVERAGE: _____

OVERALL GRADE: _____

Grade Your Goals

Complete the report card for how you would grade your CURRENT lifestyle.

Age or Grade: _____ Year: _____

SUBJECT	1ST SECTION	2ND SECTION	3RD SECTION	GRADE & AVG SCORE
FAMILY	Mother	Father	Siblings	
List score for each section				
FRIENDS	Best Friend	Classmates / Coworkers	Ext. Family (cousins, etc.)	
List score for each section				
ACTIVITIES	Hobbies	Clubs / Teams	Passion	
List score for each section				
HEALTH	Emotional / Mental	Physical	Future / Motivation	
List score for each section				
SCHOOL or WORK	Grades / Reviews	Teachers / Managers	Discipline	
List score for each section				

GRADING SCALE

A: 90-100   D: 70-73
B: 80-89   F: 0-69
C: 74-79   N/A: Not Applicable

OVERALL AVERAGE:

OVERALL GRADE:

Reflection Questions

In this section, reflect and write about why different stages of your life may have different grades.

How has your relationship with your family shifted over time?

What are the best and toughest parts of your relationship with your family?

Reflection Questions

What type of accounts do you follow on social media (celebrities, funny, motivational, etc.)? Do they have a positive impact on you?

How do you feel about the quality of friends you have? What group of people would you like to get to know better?

Reflection Questions

Of the activities you enjoy doing, what is fulfilling about them?

What do you enjoy doing that you wish you could do every day?

Reflection Questions

How often do you feel intense emotions? What reactions do you have when that happens?

What do you look forward to doing every week? Month? Year?

Reflection Questions

How do your grades or reviews line up with the effort you put into classes or work?

How has your relationship with your teachers or managers shifted over time?

Reflection Questions

Do you feel like your teachers or managers are fair? Why or why not?

Action Plan

The real first step of walking into the best versions of ourselves is knowing the areas where we can be more fulfilled. The last part of this section is creating an action plan so we can do whatever is within OUR POWER to improve those areas.

Sections in Action Plan:

Area to develop: Based on the report card and reflection question, what area do you want to work on improving right now?

What do you want this area to look like? Describe what this area of your life would look like if you could snap your fingers and have it tomorrow.

What's in my control? If you can't control something, DON'T WORRY ABOUT IT. Focusing on things out of our control stresses us out and takes energy away from what we can work on.

What's my biggest barrier? To be real, this is to just get any future excuse out of the way. We have to acknowledge whatever internal or external barrier is in the way in order to overcome it.

How will I stay accountable? Self-negotiation—not keeping promises you make to yourself—is dangerous. One person you should be able to trust is YOU. List ways to keep yourself honest with what you say you'll do.

When it's done, I will... Celebrate your wins! Regardless of if people support you, be your biggest cheerleader. (I'm cheering for you too.)

Next steps - Identify 3 areas of growth you want to target, then focus on actions you can take to get closer to your goal.

SMART Goals
Specific | Measurable | Attainable | Relevant | Time-based

Consider creating SMART goals when writing your next steps.

Action Plan

AREA TO DEVELOP #1 _____

WHAT DO I WANT THIS AREA TO LOOK LIKE?

_____

_____

_____

WHAT IS IN MY CONTROL?

_____   _____

WHAT ARE MY BIGGEST BARRIERS?

_____   _____

HOW WILL I STAY ACCOUNTABLE?

_____   _____

MY NEXT STEPS   **I will complete by:**

☐ _____   _____

☐ _____   _____

☐ _____   _____

☐ _____   _____

When it's done, I will _____

Action Plan

AREA TO DEVELOP #2 _____

WHAT DO I WANT THIS AREA TO LOOK LIKE?

_____

_____

_____

WHAT IS IN MY CONTROL?

_____   _____

WHAT ARE MY BIGGEST BARRIERS?

_____   _____

HOW WILL I STAY ACCOUNTABLE?

_____   _____

MY NEXT STEPS   **I will complete by:**

☐ _____   _____

☐ _____   _____

☐ _____   _____

☐ _____   _____

When it's done, I will _____

Action Plan

AREA TO DEVELOP #3 _____

WHAT DO I WANT THIS AREA TO LOOK LIKE?

_____

_____

_____

WHAT IS IN MY CONTROL?

_____   _____

WHAT ARE MY BIGGEST BARRIERS?

_____   _____

HOW WILL I STAY ACCOUNTABLE?

_____   _____

MY NEXT STEPS   I will complete by:

☐ _____   _____

☐ _____   _____

☐ _____   _____

☐ _____   _____

When it's done, I will _____

LEVEL 2

5 C'S OF
CONNECTION

ESTABLISHING, BUILDING, AND MAINTAINING HEALTHY RELATIONSHIPS ARE KEY. SINCE WE NEED A STRONG CIRCLE TO ELEVATE, LET'S FOCUS ON DEVELOPING TOOLS TO EFFECTIVELY CONNECT WITH PEOPLE.

CHAPTER 6
COMMUNICATION STYLE

You might already know this, but just so we start off on the same page – self-awareness is essential to success. The 1st section of the book focused on discovering what internally drives you and if your values are pointing you in the direction of your long-term vision. In this section we'll evaluate our interactions and involvement with others. In order to most effectively interact with others, build relationships, and navigate through conflict, you need to be aware of not only how others act, but also how your actions are perceived by others.

We'll start by finding out your personality type to see what patterns you may have in different situations. Lowkey, I used to hate doing stuff like this. I would think, "These tests are rigged", "They don't really know me", or "I'm one of a kind".

So, before we move forward, I want to make this clear:

I don't want you to let a label define you.

You are definitely unique, but there are also characteristics that you have in common with other people. Even though we're adaptable, we all have a natural state of being. Certain traits come more naturally to one person versus someone else. Also, people feel different levels of comfort in certain situations based on their personality type. That's what this part goes over.

We're going to start by using the Enneagram Test as an example. There are lots of different personality assessments out there – DISC Assessment, Herrmann Brain Dominance, 16 Personalities, StrengthsFinder, even Zodiac signs – but my personal favorite is the Enneagram. It breaks up personalities into 9 different categories with various scores based on how strongly we feel certain emotions, engage with people in certain situations, and the motivation behind our actions.

I suggest taking a free assessment. Here are a few free test providers online:
Truity.com/test/enneagram-personality-test
Cloverleaf.me/enneagram
Crystalknows.com/enneagram-test
Yourenneagramcoach.com

One huge benefit of these assessments is that they help us *audit our actions*.

What does *audit our actions* even mean? It means these tests help us review why we act the way we act and what drives our actions.

For example, ever since I could remember, I've been ok with spending time by myself. Honestly, I always kind of preferred it. I didn't need to have people around me often and could go a week without having small talk or text messaging friends. Since I'm satisfied with my own company, I've never been one to seek out interacting with people solely to make more friends. I'm not shy, I just was ok with my own company and being around people for too long drained my energy.

When I was older, I was introduced to the term "extrovert" and "introvert". When I heard people speak about the difference and started to do some of my own research, I saw a lot of my past actions and feelings falling in the introvert category.

Later that night in a group chat with my two sisters I typed, "Yo, I just found out what introvert means and I think I'm one of them." Their response…

"Duh! How did you not know that? You're the definition of an introvert."

I quickly learned that actions that are apparent to other people might be harder for us to realize for ourselves. Once I was fully aware of my introverted tendencies, I was also aware of the perception other people had of me. Some people thought I was standoffish, shy, or unapproachable. Instead of taking it personally and blaming others for being judgmental, I realized that was just the energy I gave off. I needed to be conscious how my natural traits were perceived by others, and how, if not used wisely, they could hold me back.

(By the way, I'm a Type 5 on the Enneagram. Type 5s are usually introverted and analytical.)

Key Characteristics Exercise

Next, we're going to explore some questions to identify some of your key characteristics.

Being _____ is most often my source of motivation. Circle 3 options.

Honorable	**Loved by Others**	**Safe & Secure**
Self-Reliant	**True to Myself**	**Productive**
At Peace	**Free**	**In Control**

My _____ is the trait I'm most proud of. Circle 3 options.

Productivity	**Calmness**	**Leadership**
Imagination	**Empathy**	**Integrity**
Liveliness	**Critical Thinking**	**Responsibility**

Other people see me as _____. Circle 3 options.

Independent   **Friendly**   **Complex**

Diligent   **Relational**   **Motivated**

Realistic   **Adventurous**   **Assertive**

I try my best to avoid _____. Circle 3 options.

Being taken advantage of   **Being selfish**   **Giving too much structure to my days**

Making non-informed decisions   **Limiting my projects**   **Saying "no" to friends**

Asking for help   **Wasting time**

Stepping into unfamiliar environments

Free Game
Don't be so attached to who you think you are.
A lot of times we're stubborn in how we portray ourselves or what our preferences have been in the past.

Reflection Questions

How can your key traits work to your benefit?

How can your key traits work to your disadvantage?

Reflection Questions

How do you think you're perceived?

How do you want to be perceived?

CHAPTER 7

CONFIDENCE

I've always been seen as the "cool" kid for as long as I can remember. Throughout school I played varsity sports, was good at talking to girls, and wore a lot of trendy clothes. I was always pretty popular. From the outside I was extremely confident...but it was for the wrong reasons. I thought that if I dressed a certain way, spoke a certain way, and was good at certain things, people would think I was cool. One summer while working at Chick-fil-A, after every paycheck I would buy a pair of sneakers that were in style. The finesse was trading "Free Sandwich" coupons for discounts on clothes. The first three weeks of school I wore 15 different pairs of shoes just to impress everyone. That's how I got my validation. Looking back, I could have bought a car, invested in my future, or done something meaningful with my money, but instead I let other people's short-term validation dictate my actions.

Real confidence sources from self-love and self-empowerment, not from the validation of others.

Being seen as the cool kid gave me a sense of value and perceived confidence, but I was really just hiding behind objects and activities instead of *being my true self*. The source of my confidence was my "status" or "accomplishments" instead of my character or complete acceptance of myself. At times, I would try to keep an image at parties or in class to the point that I couldn't even allow myself to have fun. I was so worried about what other people would think instead of being confident that I'm fine the way I am.

There was a kid in my class who would always come to school wearing "old man" clothes. He would have flower polos, boat shoes, and shorts that stopped before they reached his knees. Everyone at the time would wear expensive baggy designer jeans and t-shirts. When I approached the kid and asked him, "Hey, what makes you wear that?", he responded, "Because I like it."

He was fully comfortable in his own skin and didn't worry about what anyone thought. He was truly confident. People have a lot of respect and gravitate towards those types of people. Many people mistake something being socially acceptable with being "cool". They don't realize that something becomes "cool" once confident people do it with pride and other people just start to mimic them. There's an old phrase, "The man makes the clothes, the clothes don't make the man." In summary, it's what's on the inside that counts. Quick note – a few years later, everyone was wearing "old man" clothes and going thrift shopping. He wasn't weird or uncool, he was ahead of the curve.

Free Game
If someone lifts heavy weights and looks muscular on the outside, but eats like crap and doesn't take care of what's on the inside, how healthy are they?

You're already cool, just the way you are...just being your natural self. You can still elevate yourself in certain areas where you think you can improve, but don't let the approval of others be the source of your actions.

Confidence is the belief that you can, or can learn, to control your outcomes.

Confidence is about:

Knowing who you are

Knowing who you can become

Knowing what value you bring

Where's My Confidence Exercise

Use this exercise to help identify your unique gifts, transferable skills, and areas you can target for growth. Circle 1 – 5, whichever best describes you. 1 (Not Yet), 3 (Maybe), 5 (That's Definitely Me)

Who I Am

I'm confident I have the experience, knowledge, and expertise to learn to be effective as a leader.

1	2	3	4	5

I view failures, challenges, and barriers as fuel for personal growth.

1	2	3	4	5

I take pride and satisfaction in the successes generated by others.

1	2	3	4	5

I consistently set challenging goals and take action to achieve them.

1	2	3	4	5

I take a proactive approach to growing in my weaker areas.

1	2	3	4	5

I communicate and guide those younger than me.

1	2	3	4	5

Where's My Confidence Exercise

Who I Can Become

I continuously thrive to understand how my relationships impact my success.

| 1 | 2 | 3 | 4 | 5 |

I understand how relationships affect what goes on at school or in the workplace.

| 1 | 2 | 3 | 4 | 5 |

I am effective at persuading others to see the value of my ideas.

| 1 | 2 | 3 | 4 | 5 |

I carefully approach solving problems and creating innovative solutions.

| 1 | 2 | 3 | 4 | 5 |

I display courage and willingness to try different ways of connecting with people.

| 1 | 2 | 3 | 4 | 5 |

I represent my accomplishments and position the success of others in a compelling way.

| 1 | 2 | 3 | 4 | 5 |

Where's My Confidence Exercise

What Value I Bring

I effectively build trust with others.

1	2	3	4	5

I invest time in building trust with classmates, co-workers, and parents.

1	2	3	4	5

I have comfortable conversations with a broad variety of people.

1	2	3	4	5

I am comfortable going beyond surface level conversations with acquaintances.

1	2	3	4	5

I proactively seek to expand my circle and connect with new people.

1	2	3	4	5

I put others at ease and make them feel comfortable.

1	2	3	4	5

Reflection Questions

Review the 5 questions with the *highest* score circled above:

What do you find in common about the area of confidence these traits relate to?

How can you apply this area to uplift the people around you?

Reflection Questions

Review the 5 questions with the *lowest* scores circled above:

What do you find in common about the areas of confidence in these questions?

What steps can you take to increase your confidence in these areas?

Reflection Questions

How would an increase in confidence benefit those around you?

What obstacles will you need to manage that could get in your way?

Free Game
*"To be yourself in a world that is constantly trying to make you
something else is the greatest accomplishment."*
Ralph Waldo Emerson – American Poet

Bonus Exercise

Text 5 people close to you – "What are 3 things I'm naturally gifted at?"

Person #1:

_____   _____   _____

Person #2:

_____   _____   _____

Person #3:

_____   _____   _____

Person #4:

_____   _____   _____

Person #5:

_____   _____   _____

Sometimes others notice our gifts before we're able to see them. It helps to have people around us who can remind us of our greatness and hold us accountable to being the best version of ourselves.

Bullying

People who aren't happy or confident in themselves try to bring other people down. I've learned this from not only dealing with people who I felt like were trying to come at me, but from looking myself in the mirror and realizing that I used to be a bully sometimes.

There's a phrase that says "hurt people, hurt people". You can't give what you don't have. People who are happy with themselves, spread love. People who are hurting, spread pain.

I know you have probably been through tough times at some point in your life. After seeing my pops lose his temper, I realized that he would react that way because he had a lot of painful experiences. His hurt caused him to express those emotions by lashing out. And when I would get mad at other people or felt the need to prove myself through flexing my power, I realized it was because of my own insecurities. In the end, I just felt worse. Especially when I did it to people I love. Working on my insecurities and finding my real confidence allowed me to create healthy relationships with both strangers and those close to me.

CHAPTER 8

COMMUNITY

George Floyd was murdered on May 25, 2020. A few weeks earlier, the video of Ahmaud Arbery being chased down and shot in Georgia, my home state, surfaced in the news. Seeing both of the murders clearly on video had an effect on most people, but as a Black man and as someone who has been profiled time and time again, their deaths deeply impacted me. I could relate to them on a different level. It not only made me angry, but it also scared me. When I thought of Breonna Taylor being shot in her apartment while she was asleep, it gave me flashbacks of my own encounters when the cameras were off and nobody would listen to my story.

I went to share my thoughts on Twitter and reshare posts on Instagram, but I knew most of my followers agreed with my views. I didn't feel like I was doing enough. That's when an idea came to mind: *Directly communicate with people I see as different from me.*

I've benefited from the privilege of attending extremely diverse schools and building friendships with people of various cultures, races, and generations. I'm a part of a lot of different communities, the Black community, the business community, the Christian community, my alumni community, the Georgia community, and as an American, even the community of the United States of America.

Once I reached out to people from my business community who didn't have much of a connection with the Black community, I was able to educate them on how many people in the Black community were feeling. To my surprise, even though they knew other Black people, they never had a deep conversation about their unique experience as a Black person. Knowing the diverse experiences of people not only helps to connect communities, but allows them to grow even stronger.

Community and communication have the same Latin root word – communis. Communis means "common, public, shared by all or many". In order to build a strong community, we have to first connect on what we have in common, then be willing to learn about how differences can affect others in our community.

Diversity isn't only about race. It can include religion, gender, sexual orientation, age, socio-economic status, physical disability, or other demographic differences. This section will focus on the importance of diversity, equity, and inclusion, as well as the need to get out of our comfort zones to truly embrace the experiences of others within our community.

Here's a comparison between the terms:

Diversity ➡ Having **different people** at the table.

Equity ➡ People having a **proportional amount** at the table.

Inclusion ➡ People **feeling welcomed** at the table.

You can substitute "table" for school, company, or country to paint a picture.

Why is diversity important?

Different types of people bring different perspectives, ideas, and add more value to a community. When you listen to a band, do they all play the same instrument, the same way, at the same tempo? In order to give a crowd the best experience, the band has to have musicians that all bring something different to the table. Those differences have to be acknowledged in order to capitalize on their unique contribution. Diversity is a strength. If it's not seen and celebrated, then a community won't grow through the power of diverse ideas.

Why is equity important?

I'm one of the youngest cousins in my family. If you have older cousins or siblings, you probably know the pain when it comes to "sharing" with them. Whenever my aunt would come home with food, my older cousin would push me to the side and take all of the good stuff. Since they could over power me, I was either always left with less or something not as good. Even though we were under the same roof and the same opportunity was on the table, I knew I didn't have a fair shot because of something I couldn't control.

This is how a lot of groups in different communities are treated. Circumstances that they couldn't control put them in a more difficult situation than other groups. They start with a disadvantage. Equity is important because it ensures that those who start with a disadvantage gain additional opportunities to even the playing field.

Why is inclusion important?

Did you ever give someone the silent treatment or get the silent treatment yourself? It's trash! You hear people having conversations, you're in the room, but you might as well be somewhere else. It gets to the point where you just give up and sit down in your corner.

If someone is invited somewhere but doesn't feel welcomed or heard, we can't expect to benefit from having them there. The beauty of diversity within a community is that we get to grow with innovative ideas from different perspectives, but if the people with the new insights are silenced, the purpose is defeated.

What can we do to build community and promote diversity, equity, and inclusion?

The first thing we need to do is acknowledge that a problem exists. It's impossible to improve anything if we won't say that something is wrong with it. Nothing is perfect, but the inability to admit that things need to get better doesn't help anyone in the long run.

The second thing we can do is call out our own implicit biases. Implicit bias is the unconscious process we use to categorize groups of people. It's natural that everyone has some type of bias that effects their initial thoughts about a person or situation. They may automatically associate a job to a specific gender, assume a person uses a certain pronoun, or even hear a story and make a character up in their head.

Even though it may be weird or make us feel guilty to say it out loud, we have to first admit that we have a bias in order for it to be fixed. It doesn't make you a bad person to recognize how your upbringing, environment, or the media you've watched affects how you see the world. However, bias can turn into a problem if you can't come to terms with how it affects you. Also, it will make it impossible to build a healthy community with people different from you.

The third thing we can do is not take offense to other people's struggles. Most people can see someone who is blind and instantly empathize with their disadvantage. Even though they still have the ability to be successful, the world's inaccessibility through its structure has made their life harder. Privilege has become a touchy word. Privilege really just means that you don't have to deal with a problem that someone else experiences. I'm not blind so I have the privilege of being able to see. Everyone has certain privilege based on benefits they didn't control. Instead of feeling guilty about the privileges we have, we can empathize with the difficulties other people go through. By being empathetic and recognizing our privilege, we can discover ways to help other communities, even if they have problems we don't experience.

Find the 1%, then put 100% into that.

We all have something in common with somebody. Even if there are 99 differences, there's 1 thing we can connect on. After you find that 1 thing to connect on, focus on seeing the good in that person and how you relate. Sometimes it's sharing an interest in sports, religion, or other hobbies. From there it creates comfortability and reminds us that regardless of our differences, we're all human. Once a relationship grows, it creates a space to have conversations about differences in the human experience, learn another vantage point, and share a perspective on what goes on in our world.

Reflection Questions

You meet a random person on the street who looks completely different from you. What are 5 subjects that you could bring up where you could have a mutual interest or connection?

What are 5 categories you associate with your identity or communities you're associated with?

Reflection Questions

What are 3 ways you've been privileged?

How can you use your privilege to empower others?

Have you ever felt like you've been left out? If yes, how could others have made you feel more welcomed?

CHAPTER 9

CONFLICT

MANAGEMENT

Conflict – having a disagreement with someone or something – is going to happen. It might happen every day. Whether with a classmate, sibling, parent, significant other, or person driving in the car next to you, you're going to experience conflict. Even if you try your best to avoid it, it'll eventually find you.

That's not a bad thing though. Conflict can often times help us build patience, learn more about ourselves, and find out how to make the most out of certain relationships. Since we know conflict is eventually going to come our way, it's important to prepare for those moments. Once you're prepared for anything, the situation doesn't seem as scary.

If you've ever been part of a team, you know conflict is in your face almost every day. Even if you have the same goals, you and your teammates may not be on the same page with things, and still have to find a solution.

At one of my previous jobs, I had 4 teammates. Micah, Chris, Sarah, and Laura. When conflict shows itself, people tend to fall into four different categories. The four teammates I had all fell into different categories whenever there was a disagreement between us:

Four Modes of Conflict

Competing | Compromising | Avoiding | Collaborating

Micah would go into a **competitive** mode. He would strongly state his points and would rarely budge on what he thought. His goal was primarily to prove that he had the best idea and wasn't necessarily interested in hearing other solutions.

Chris would go into **compromise** mode. He wasn't as assertive as Micah, but still made sure his point was clear. He came into the conversation willing to listen, as long as he got some solid input on how to move forward from the conflict.

Sarah would try to **avoid** any conflict. Instead of engaging like Micah and Chris, she would stay quiet in hopes that people wouldn't talk about the disagreement until it fizzled out. Whatever outcome the team came up with, she would say it was fine.

Laura would think of ways to **collaborate** when conflict on the team arose. She could go head-to-head with Micah whenever he would press his point, but would take what everyone would say into consideration so we could find a creative solution.

Each of my teammates had benefits and areas to monitor when it came to the way they handled conflict. There's no right or wrong in whichever person you resonate with. The secret is being aware of which mode you naturally revert to, how it can affect the situation, and transition to a different mode to get the best result moving forward.

Here are some natural skills and potential issues for each mode of conflict:

Micah was able to make quick decisions during times of conflict since he was confident in his choice. This is needed when people are hesitant to take action on hard decisions that need to be made. I would also always want Micah on my side during a debate. Micah just had to be cautious of possibly turning into a bully or manipulating others to get his way.

Chris was great at negotiating and finding a middle ground. By clearly knowing the value he wanted to get out the situation, he was able to agree on a solution without giving up what was most important to him. Chris' negotiating could transition into solely considering himself and neglecting his team if he wasn't careful.

Sarah had the ability to push low priority conversations to the side when more important things needed to be handled. When the topic isn't that serious to the end goal, there's no need to engage in a drawn-out debate. Sarah had to make sure she didn't let topics that were important to her go unaddressed to the point where she was silently frustrated.

Lauren made everyone feel like they were heard during confrontations. By identifying everyone's concerns, we were usually able to take the best parts of everyone's view to see the situation in a different light. Lauren had to be aware of when she was over monitoring situations instead of letting them resolve naturally.

I used to be the guy who would never back down from a fight. If I ever felt like I was being disrespected, I felt the need to make sure they knew "I'm not the one."

One time while I was playing intramural basketball, there was a guy on the other team who was being really aggressive towards me and my teammates. I had seen him do this to people in the previous weeks and thought, "He better not come my way." After our game, a spectator approached me and asked how the game went since he arrived late. I told him we won, but there was a dude on the other team who was trippin and pointed him out.

Once he saw me point in his direction, he headed over to confront me. My "I'm not the one" mentality started to creep in. When he stepped up, he got in my face to ask what I said about him. I gave him a slick reply.

After my reply, he immediately pushed me. At this point, I was in too deep. I felt like I was disrespected since he put his hands on me, and wasn't going to let him shove me and get away with it. I immediately let my fist fly into his jaw and saw blood fly out his mouth as his body fell to the floor. As I got in a fighting stance waiting for him to stand up, a few of my teammates ran to pull me back.

A lot of times, we feel like we have to fight once we get into a conflict. After having to go to court for fighting, getting arrested, paying to get bailed out of jail while I was broke, and having a battery charge on my record, I learned the hard way that we have the power to approach tense situations in a healthy way so we can avoid ending up in heated conflict.

In this situation, the first mistake I made was playing myself. Internally, I told myself since I didn't say anything directly to him, I wasn't starting the conflict. But in reality, I knew better. My actions, whether directly towards him or not, could have been different. I didn't have to point towards him or even acknowledge he existed. But since I was mad at how he treated me and my teammates, I let my emotions get the best of me.

Another mistake I made was engaging when he approached me. I had the choice to ignore him, but I didn't. Pride is a tricky emotion. It can make you feel like you need to prove yourself to people who don't matter. I felt the need to say something slick to him, when in reality I could have walked away. If we really don't care what someone thinks, there's no need to prove anything to them. To help avoiding making the same mistakes I now ask myself a few questions.

5 Questions to Ask During a Conflict

Is it worth it right now?

Sometimes, avoiding the conflict is the best approach. If it's not that deep, there's no reason to put our energy towards it. We have to just let it go. If it's pride that's driving us, then we should work on internally finding peace with who we are so we don't have to prove it to anyone else. That comes with developing confidence.

Where is my power?

No matter how much you practice, conflict can be frustrating. It can be especially difficult if we feel like we can't do anything that matters to help our cause. By focusing on our power in the situation, as opposed to what other people are doing or ways we're limited, we can come up with a solution that moves the needle closer to getting what we need or want.

What do I want to get out of this?

Sometimes conflict arises just from miscommunication or lack of clarity. By making it clear to ourselves what we want, it does two things:

1. It helps us clearly be able to tell others what we want, so there's less confusion.
2. It helps us realize if what we want is unreasonable or just an ego boost.

If we realize the situation has gotten to a point where we have what we need, there's no real reason we need to engage in conflict. If our goal is to just get the person to admit we're right, then we're moving out of ego and it can damage the relationship even further.

What do they to get out of this?

Have you ever been in an argument with someone, just to realize y'all really want the same end goal? This also can happen when there isn't clarity between the two parties. One way it can be solved is by asking what their goal is, as opposed to making assumptions. By asking, we can clearly let them know whether we're capable of meeting their needs or not.

What's the root cause of the conflict?

People often have arguments about surface level topics when there is really a deeper issue that needs to be addressed. If you find yourself constantly getting into disagreements with someone you care about, find an outside party to help you both dig deeper to find out where the source of the tension lies. They say it's tough to see the picture when you're in the frame. It's helpful to have an outside perspective to reveal a different point of view.

This section was purposely titled *Conflict Management* instead of *Conflict Resolution*. Like we mentioned before, conflict is going to arise. It's healthy to address conflict to move forward in the relationship or with your life as a whole. Moving forward is the key though. Sometimes, there may not be a clear resolution. At times, the conflict will be too complex to solve. When that's the case, we just have to do our best to work around the issues, accept that you have a different point of view, agree to disagree, and move forward in the best way possible.

Reflection Questions

Whenever a situation between group members, siblings, or coworkers gets really heated, which person at the beginning of the chapter do you relate to the most?

What have people pointed out to you about how you handle conflict?

When was the last time a conflict arose in your life? Why was it necessary to engage in the conflict?

What could you have done differently in that situation?

CHAPTER 10
CRUCIAL
CONVERSATIONS

Tough conversations have always been right in my face and I was never one to back down. Whether they have been around race, heart to heart conversations concerning distrust, or someone on my team not performing well. When I was younger, my parents made some mistakes that had an impact on me. Instead of avoiding the situation, I would find myself setting the table to have a hard conversation. Not only did it clear the air and strengthen our relationship, it prepared me to have crucial conversations with people in different areas of my life.

Free Game
Avoiding the hard conversations doesn't help anyone in the long run.

Avoiding talking about subjects because they may feel awkward or emotional can drag the problem out. This can lead to resentment or more problems in relationships.

There is an art to having crucial conversations. Naturally, I'm a blunt person. My blunt delivery has hurt some people's feelings in the past.

Instead of hiding behind the response "I'm just being honest" or "their reaction isn't my responsibility", I learned it was my responsibility to deliver the message in a loving way. Now, I try to consciously consider what their reaction may be, reflect on my delivery, and take responsibility for how I contribute to the conversation.

10 Tips on Having Effective Crucial Conversations

1. If they know your energy, they won't question your intentions.

It's very important to come to the conversation in the right mindset. Have you ever been around someone and you can instantly tell that they're mad? The energy is awkward and you can feel the tension. It doesn't provide a great environment to talk about touchy topics. Before you walk into a tough conversation, make sure your mind is right. If you need to go to a quiet place or feed yourself some positive vibes, then take the time to do that so you arrive with positive energy.

Do you tend to rush into conversations or wait for the right moment?

What is your process before having a tough conversation?

2. Provide a frame work.

People in a crucial conversation often times feel nervous before it starts. They're anxious at what topics will come up or if they'll offend someone, especially in group settings. By beginning with a clear introduction on what you want to discuss, why it is a relevant concern, and how the conversation can be structured – i.e. "I wanted to share how I felt about (insert situation) and then hear your perspective" – as opposed to jumping into the conversation with how you feel, it provides context so they know what to expect and aren't caught off guard.

What could someone say to you before a hard conversation to ease your nerves?

How have you initiated hard conversations in the past?

3. Be clear on the goal.

Write out what you want to get out of the conversation. Sometimes, we just want to state how we feel without having a real goal in mind. This can cause a two-way conversation to turn into a one-sided vent session.

If you can't state a reasonable goal, or the goal is only to voice your feelings without the other person being able to make an actionable change to help the situation, it may be best to reevaluate whether talking to them versus a counselor is a better approach.

Have you ever finished a long conversation and felt like there was no progress?

If so, why did you feel that way?

4. Write out a script.

When a topic is deeply emotional to you but may not have the same effect on the other person, it can get frustrating. Emotions can take over and before we know it, we're in tears because our message isn't being received like we hoped. Writing out a script on the points you want to make, potential push back responses, and how you can reply to those responses can help us control our first reactions. By rehearsing the script, it not only eases our anxiety about having the conversation through practicing, but it allows us to stick with articulating facts about the situation and not allowing feelings of anger, hurt, or fear to take over.

Are your thoughts clearer when you journal them out?

Have you ever talked to yourself in the mirror to gain confidence?

5. Call UP instead of Call OUT.

Calling out someone is when we shame, guilt, or embarrass someone into making a change. *"You can't be that dumb." "You'll never make it doing that." "You're just like your daddy."* Calling out can make them feel inferior and cause more conflict.

Calling up someone is when we uplift them so they feel empowered to make a change. *"I know you can do it." "You have so much potential." "I want to see the best for you."* Calling up leads to the person feeling valued and shows that you have their best interest in mind.

Even though both ways are meant to motivate, the push can be delivered in a loving way.

How do you like people to encourage you?

What's the most uplifting words someone has said to you?

How would it feel to be on the other side of your feedback?

6. W.A.I.T. (Why Am I Talking?)

When we are focusing on what to say next instead of focusing on listening, we can't learn any new information. Sometimes the best response is to listen, wait, then ask a question. Our words should have a purpose that's productive to the conversation. By waiting patiently and listening, we can pick up on how the other person is thinking and better communicate when we do speak.

On a scale of 1-10 (you can't say 7), how well do you listen?

What percentage of the talking do you do during tough conversations?

7. Less is more.

Messages get lost in translation when topics are over explained. Clear and concise messaging will help you make your point without losing your audience along the way. You can do this by starting with the simplest explanation. If they get the message, cool! Goal accomplished. If they need more explaining, then give them small chunks at a time. Once they understand your point, you don't want to confuse them by continuing to explain. The most memorable taglines are short and to the point for a reason.

How often do you find yourself going on rants?

8. Go to the source.

Did you ever play the game Telephone as a child? If you haven't, kids sit in a large circle next to their classmates and someone thinks of a sentence. The person who created the sentence, whispers it to the person next to them, that person whispers it to the person next to them, and the cycle continues. By the time the message gets to the last kid, it normally comes out completely different than how it originated.

Conversations on difficult topics work the same way. If you go to the source of the issue with what's causing you concern, it helps prevent the message from getting distorted. Plus, people respect someone who confronts them more than someone who talks behind their back.

How comfortable are you at going to "the source"?

9. Ask permission to interrupt.

There are times when someone else is talking and we either get confused, overwhelmed, or just want to move to the next topic. Interrupting someone during a passionate conversation can cause tension if it's not done with care. When you ask someone permission to give your perspective, then it comes off less assertive and still allows you a chance to talk. A few ways to phrase the question are:

"Can I share an observation?"

"Do you mind if I make sure we're on the same page?"

10. The Right Channel.

You can't use a hammer to fix a broken phone screen. A pair of Jordan shoes won't do any good if you're playing in a hockey rink. We need to use the correct tool in order to fix a specific problem.

Social media, text, email, phone calls, video chat, and in-person conversations are all valuable ways to communicate. But we have to make sure we use the right channel at the right time to ensure that the message keeps its value. Social media, text, and email are great for quick or simple conversations, but can feel impersonal or get confusing for more complicated conversations. Phone calls, video chat, and in-person conversations are more effective when emotions are in-play since you can feel someone's energy, but can become overwhelming if used too often. Considering what channel is most appropriate for specific conversations helps to get your message across in a productive way.

What channel do you normally use to communicate?

How can you determine when is best to use a different channel?

What channel are you most hesitant of using for a tough conversation?

Free Game
Change the delivery, not the message.

One of the greatest coaches of all time is Coach Krzyzewski (known as Coach K). He's been the Duke Men's Basketball Team coach for decades, coached multiple USA Olympic Teams with Kobe Bryant, LeBron James, and Steph Curry to gold medals, and is greatly respected by most people in the sports community. When he was asked how he continues to connect with his players from different generations, he said that he never changes what he says, but knows he has to change how he says it.

In order to have meaningful and effective crucial conversations, we have to focus on delivering the message in the best way someone can receive it rather than how we would like to give it.

Reflection Questions

When have you had to deliver difficult feedback? How did it turn out?

Did you successfully deliver the feedback? How could you tell?

LEVEL 3

MENTAL HEALTH M.A.G.I.C.

PERSONAL DEVELOPMENT IS A NEVER-ENDING CYCLE. IN ORDER TO BE SUSTAINABLY HAPPY, WE'LL NEED TO ADDRESS OUR EMOTIONAL WELLNESS THROUGHOUT OUR JOURNEY.

CHAPTER 11
MINDFULNESS

I used to get jealous when I would hear people talk about their relationship with their dads, especially when I was younger. My pops always had a hard time controlling his emotions. When I was little, he would yell and curse whenever he lost his temper, which seemed like it was all the time. I would get so mad to the point I would cry, but knew I couldn't do anything about it. The jealousy would come from having my dad around, but still not feeling as connected as my friends were with their dads or stepdads.

One day after my parents finally separated, my mom invited my dad over to try to talk things out as a family. During the conversation, my dad got mad and instantly let his anger get the best of him again. That's when I was introduced to the importance of mindfulness.

Mindfulness is being able to acknowledge your emotions, but not letting them control your reactions.

It's perfectly fine to feel angry, offended, sad, disappointed, anxious, whatever...but making a quick and emotional reaction is dangerous. Whether the reaction is to internally panic or get into an unnecessary argument, taking a moment to take a step back, breathe, address how we are feeling, and decide how to move forward is a great practice.

Don't sit in it.

The first step to practicing mindfulness is self-awareness. Learning to honestly explore our emotions, reasons that we are feeling them, then eventually discovering how our mindset can shift to decrease our stress level is the goal. The emotions that we feel are very real, but the unconscious reason we give ourselves to feel that emotion may not be true.

For example - my girlfriend might not text me back on a Friday night. The emotion I could possibly feel ranges from anxiety to disappointment to anger. Me *feeling* that emotion is *real. The made-up scenarios*—from thinking that she is with another guy to wondering if she is stranded somewhere because she ran out of gas—I came up with in my head that fueled those emotions though *aren't necessarily true.*

All I've done is stress myself out by continuing to feed into the imaginary narrative instead of pausing to see why I am feeling the way I am feeling.

Questions to Stop Emotional Reactions

1. **What emotion am I feeling? Why?**

   Identify the emotion and the trigger.

2. **What are the facts?**

   Separate "how you feel" about what happened (opinion on another person's attitude or tone, future outcome, intentions, etc.) from the undisputable facts (specific words spoken, physical actions, etc.).

3. **What could I clarify?**

   Once you decipher between fact and opinion, decide whether gaining clarity on ambiguous details would be helpful to making a conclusion.

4. **What is the best way to move forward?**

   The first reaction isn't necessarily the best reaction. Taking a moment to reflect on the best way to move forward helps prevent regret later on. We don't have to instantly label a situation as "good" or "bad" Sometimes, it's best to just wait and do nothing.

Reframing is another way we can address what we tell ourselves to reduce our stress. *Reframing is looking at a situation from a different angle*. At first the situation may seem negative, but reframing allows us to focus on the situation from a more positive perspective.

Examples:

If only 3 people liked my Instagram, I might go from:
"I suck, no one likes my content."

"I'm glad I got out my comfort zone and I'm learning what my audience appreciates."

If my teacher says I'm not working hard, I might go from:
"He's a hater and doesn't like me."

"He must really think I have potential to be better."

Get Help Healing

Therapy and counseling are ways to have someone who is trained help us reflect on our emotions by asking us questions that give us a different perspective, which allows us to reframe our thought process.

A common mistake is to think that because a situation is typical or part of our norm, then it shouldn't have an effect on us. My dad getting angry and saying mean things seemed typical to me. It seemed normal. But I learned that even though it happened often, I was still affected in ways I didn't notice. Getting used to the pain doesn't mean a scar isn't there. Some wounds are invisible and still need to go through a healing process. Everyone goes through trauma in different ways. That's not your fault. But as we get older, it's our responsibility to seek help to try to get healing so we can be the best versions of ourselves.

Reflection Questions

Has there been a time when something happened that first seemed negative, but a positive experience, lesson, or outcome eventually came from it?

What is an "invisible wound" that you are healing from? What steps are taking to help the healing?

CHAPTER 12
ATTITUDE

I'm coming in hot!

First off – You're in control!

You control your vision.
You control your energy.
You control your reactions.
You control how you move forward.

Second off - You always have a choice.

And normally – the choice is simple, even if it's not easy.

You can choose:

To blame other people ➡️ *or* Focus on your power

What's easy now ➡️ *or* What helps you in the future

Making excuses ➡️ *or* Making adjustments

When I was in school, everybody wore NIKE t-shirts with catchy sayings on them. One of the shirts that got popular said "Lazy but Talented" printed across the front. Lazy but talented...even though it was just supposed to be a cool t-shirt, dudes that wore the shirt really took it to heart. They were the students who wouldn't really put effort into anything. Whether it was sports or school, they would either always have an excuse about why they didn't do something or would pretend like they didn't care. At first, I thought, "Ok, that activity just isn't important to them," but as I kept paying attention, I saw that they were just scared. They chose to be lazy because they were scared of not being good at something. They wouldn't try on any of their assignments because they were scared of failing. They were scared of what people would think if they put in effort and weren't instantly good. They were scared to feel embarrassed.

It's scary trying to do something that's hard. I'm not going to lie. Even to this day, when I come across something I don't know how to do off the cuff, I start to second guess myself. I start to think, "Maybe I should just avoid it."

But you know what I started to realize? I have a choice.

I can do what seems easy right now and tell myself, "Oh well, I'm just gonna give up and not try" or I can get out my comfort zone, stop making excuses, and take on whatever it is head on. That's the only way you level up. When I looked around at where older dudes were who didn't take school seriously, I didn't want to be them, straight up. I saw where they ended up because the truth was, they were scared. A lot of them were smart, they were "Lazy but Talented". And because they were scared to even try, they ended up not going anywhere.

You have the chance to level up and elevate your lifestyle. You have the chance to be the first in your family to accomplish goals your grandparents wouldn't have imagined. You have the chance to break generational curses. And it all starts with focusing on what you can control - *Your Attitude.*

In this section, we'll specifically focus on:

Affirmations: Controlling your energy proactively.

Forgiveness: Controlling your energy retroactively.

Free Game
"When life puts you in tough situations, don't say 'Why me?' just say 'Try me'."
Dwayne "The Rock" Johnson – Actor & Former Wrestler

Affirmations

After going through a tough week when I was feeling unhappy, trapped, and confused on what was next, I asked one of my good friends how he kept a smile on his face every day. He told me about always starting his day off with a morning routine. In addition to waking up early, working out, reviewing his goals, reading his Bible, and having quiet time before the chaos of the work day, he wrote daily affirmations. Affirmations are just positive statements we tell ourselves. The affirmations helped to mentally prepare him prior to battling with whatever adversity was thrown his way for the day. He knew that negative energy and insecurities could seep into his mind and kill his vibe, so the daily affirmations served as a reminder before he stepped into the world.

To be real, I used to think affirmations were corny. Repeating words to myself over and over didn't seem appealing. But to keep it 100, it's one of the most transformative activities I've done to reframe my mindset and protect my energy.

A few of my favorite affirmations are:

- I love being out of my comfort zone.
- I am bright and brilliant.
- I will not take anything personally.
- I am handsome and confident.

Personally, I have a total of 12 affirmations that I read or write in the morning.

Free Game
Remember the power of words and how they can affect your day. Negative words can ruin it, but positive words can elevate it.

Create Your Affirmations

Now, it's your turn to create your own affirmations. They don't have to be super philosophical.

Here's a framework to start:
Characteristics or traits you love about yourself (I am...)
Thoughts or actions you want to achieve today (I will...)
What you would tell yourself to keep going.

I am _____

I am _____

I am _____

I am _____

I will _____

I will _____

I will _____

I will _____

I _____

I _____

Forgiveness

Forgiveness is the best way to control your energy. Whether it's forgiving yourself, forgiving close ones, or forgiving strangers, making the choice to not let past pain control your current attitude allows for you to have peace.

Let me break it down.

There was this guy who I ended up fighting in school. We were in the library and I felt like he was being disrespectful to me and my girlfriend. After our altercation, we would randomly see each other...which was awkward. I still felt some type of way whenever I saw him and instantly got into a weird mood.

One day, I went into the bathroom and there he was. It was just me and him. I was on edge about if we were going to fight again or pretend like each other didn't exist. That's when the little voice in my head told me "Kam, just let it go. Forgive him". I apologized to him for how the fight went down and told him there were no hard feeling. And to my surprise, he told me thanks and that it meant a lot.

I realized that other people's reactions really don't have much to do with us, but with what they are going through at the time. I'm not saying what he did was ok, but I did realize that I couldn't let his actions have a hold on me. He's human and makes mistakes just like I do. I realized continuing to stay mad at him was just making my life harder. I was letting him control my energy by not allowing myself to move on from the situation.

Write down 3 people who you haven't forgiven.

_____ _____ _____

Do you want them to take up room in your head?

The truth is, you're not always going to see eye to eye or instantly get along with someone. But the only way you can move forward is to forgive. If you won't forgive someone, drop it, and keep moving, otherwise they still have control.

CHAPTER 13
GRATITUDE

When COVID hit us in 2020, everything took a pause. Students couldn't go to school. People couldn't go to work. Slowly, we started to see people lose their jobs, sense of normalcy, and even their lives. There was a lot going on that left people feeling depressed, disheartened, and not looking forward to the future. The only way to get our mind off of everything that was going wrong was to focus on everything that was going well. We had to focus on the positive.

Gratitude fixes negativity. It's the ability to appreciate everything you've had in the past, currently have, and look forward to having in the future. Gratitude is a choice and an action. Its deciding to focus on the gifts and the possibilities, and taking the time to give thanks, whether big or small. Gratitude fixes negativity because our mind is now happy that we are in a better situation than we could be if things were different. Gratitude helps us realize that we are literally living someone else's dream.

It's essential to be content with what you have you in life in order to ever be happy. Content is just a fancy word for fulfilled. There were times in life when I made more money than I ever expected to when I was younger, but still wasn't happy. The reason I wasn't happy was because I didn't fully appreciate everything I had before the money came. I thought that another object or accomplishment was what I needed to be happy. But I already had what I needed; I just didn't realize it.

Have you ever been on a vacation? I've had the chance to go to Disney World a few times. They call it the "happiest place on Earth." There are thousands of people from different backgrounds, income-levels, and life circumstances. They all come to Disney World to have a good time. When you get there, it can be crazy crowded. You can wait in lines for up to an hour while you wait for your ride. In order to reduce the wait time, the theme park created the FastPass. The FastPass allows you to go in a line with less people so you can get on the ride faster.

So, if someone is at Disney World without the FastPass and they see someone with the FastPass get to the ride faster than they do, should they be unhappy? NO! That would be so silly. They're already at Disney World, the happiest place on Earth, and would just ruin their time if they constantly focused on what they didn't have as opposed to enjoying the moment.

Is it ok for someone to still want to get a FastPass next time they come and save up to buy one? Of course! One of my mentors told me, "Always be grateful, but never settle." What he means is even though we should be fulfilled with what we have, it doesn't mean we can't strive for more. It just means that I'll be happy whether I get it or not. Don't be dependent on getting a FastPass to enjoy your life.

Enjoying the moment can be a hard concept when we feel like things just aren't falling in our favor. I was working at a large company and had started to really build my reputation. Even though I was located in Atlanta, my work had gotten me recognition at our headquarters in New York City. Everyone told me in order to elevate in my career, I would have to eventually get a job in New York.

After getting a call that they wanted me to interview for a position that opened up at the headquarters, it looked like my New York move was on the way. I was friends with the lady in charge of the whole department and had previously helped on a few projects that impressed them. After a few phone conversations, they asked if they could fly me to New York to meet the team.

I spent the day in New York being shown around the headquarters and meeting all of the senior leadership. They kept telling me all the benefits of the job, living in New York, and how the position could help my career. It seemed like they were trying to convince me to take the job more than I was actually being interviewed to get it! When I flew back, they told me they would contact me next week to give me the next steps.

I walked in the next Tuesday to see an email in my inbox - "Dear Kameron, we regret to inform you that you have not been selected as a candidate for the position." I was crushed. All of my hard work seemed like it was for nothing. I felt stuck in my situation in Atlanta and didn't see a way out because this door was shut in my face. I instantly felt the need to judge the moment.

In order to live in the moment, we can't always judge the moment we're currently in as "good" or "bad". We just have to live in it. I thought that not getting the position in New York was terrible, but it was actually great. A few months later, another position came up that I liked better and paid even more. Instead of instantly bringing myself down for things not going my way, I've learned to appreciate whatever situation I'm in. We never know what the next chapter has in store.

Service has a close relationship with gratitude.

Have you ever volunteered before? It could be feeding the homeless, helping building a house, or going to visit a hospital. In most of those cases, we are taking time to help people who need something that we may take for granted. A meal, a place to live, or good health. Not only does serving those people help remind us of how fortunate we are, but it also leaves us with a sense of fulfillment from adding value to someone else's life.

Giving effort, time, or our talents to serve and provide value to others helps your mental health. By feeding into others and using your overflow of resources to fill other people's cup, it will leave you feeling fulfilled.

Free Game
"It's not what you get in this world, it's what you give."
Nipsey Hussle – Rapper, Activist, Entrepreneur

Exercise

Let's reflect on what you're grateful for. List 3 things in the following categories. You can reflect on this list whenever you're feeling down or even start off the day reading it to give yourself perspective.

Personal Life or Family

_____   _____   _____

Belongings (Home, objects)

_____   _____   _____

Friends/Community

_____   _____   _____

Physical Health

_____   _____   _____

Emotional/Spiritual Health

_____   _____   _____

Talents/Intellectual Skills

_____   _____   _____

Reflection Questions

What's the most important action you've taken to serve others?

How can you serve others that are less fortunate than you in the future?

CHAPTER 14
INSPIRATION

Motivation can make you start, but inspiration helps you continue. Let me break it down.

Motivation is an outside force pushing you. You need an external motive. It could be money if you do well. It could be a punishment if you do bad. Motivation is something that triggers temporary emotion to give you a boost. It's not a negative thing – I even appreciate motivation when I need a kick, but its temporary.

In this section, we'll focus on inspiration. That internal push that keeps you going during the hard times.

During my lowest point in life, I was depressed and suicidal. I hadn't resolved a lot of traumas from the past and it weighed on me heavy. It got to the point where I really felt like I couldn't take it anymore and didn't think I was supposed to be here. The only thought that saved me was - *My life matters and I have a purpose bigger than me.*

Life is hard. Point blank. If you don't have a vision for why you're doing something, you can end up feeling like your actions, maybe even your existence, are pointless. But – YOU ARE WORTHY. YOU DO HAVE A PURPOSE. Even if we lose sight of it or can't see it in the moment.

Inspiration comes from discovering what matters to us. It confirms we're part of something that matters. It's that internal pull that comes from within. But where do we start in finding inspiration? We start by exploring our purpose. Finding your purpose is just that...*finding* it. You have to explore...it takes effort. Purpose never has to do with ourselves. Its bigger than that. It's about impacting others and answering our calling.

Who are you called to impact?

This is the question I had to ask myself. *Why am I supposed to be here?* I used to have this thought when I was depressed. The hardest part about this question is... **You won't find the answer immediately.**

I wish I could say otherwise, but it's the truth. I'll be real. Not knowing is tough at times, but that's why we have to take time to create our vision. It gives us a target. The fact that you can see it in your mind means that IT'S POSSIBLE. We can only find our purpose if we hang in there long enough for it to reveal itself.

My inspiration started from a change in perspective. After my life was spared from a suicide attempt, I began addressing all of the trauma I ignored for so long. I started investing in learning more about myself and facing the skeletons in my closet. As I continued to address my past pain, my purpose started to reveal itself.

In a small reflection group, I felt an internal pull to share an experience where I was sexually abused as a child. As I was telling the story, the group got silent. I didn't know what to expect when I was finished. All of a sudden, one of the girls in the group spoke up. "Dang. The same thing happened to me, but I've never told anyone." Another guy in the group spoke up, "I was sexually assaulted too."

At that point I realized - *There is purpose in our pain.*

- What if I told you that you were meant to change lives?
- What if I told you that you are an inspiration to a younger version of yourself?
- Would that make you feel like you matter? Like you're supposed to be here?

Well...you are meant to change lives! You are meant to be an inspiration to others. You do matter.

Whatever pain you're going through, has a purpose. The pain you went though, can help heal others if you heal yourself. It's your choice to use the pain for your purpose. It could be solving a problem other people haven't addressed. It could be fixing an issue you see your family struggle with. It could be being an example of someone who persevered to give other people hope. You could be the spark to change a life, to change the world. *That sounds like inspiration to keep going.*

A few important things to consider when looking for both motivation or inspiration:

Whatever fills our mind, feeds our thoughts.

What we absorb in our mind is important. Not only the people we're around, but music, podcast, books, who we follow on social media…all of those feed into our mental. When we're feeding our mind positive energy with productive content, it makes it that much easier to stay positive, focused on our vision, and excited to pursue everything in our future.

Make moves out of love, not survival.

I love myself and hope you love yourself too. When we love ourselves, we should desire the best for ourselves and let that be the motive for our actions. Fear can cripple us to not pursue things that will only help us uplift ourselves. Loving yourself and loving others requires us to get out of our comfort zone. Love conquers fear in the end.

We find what we look for.

If you have your mind made up that negative things will happen, that's what you'll see. But if you look for the good, that's what you'll find. Have you ever been around someone who is just always complaining? It's tough to get excited around them because they're going to point out something that will bring you down. That's how finding inspiration works. You can't find what you don't look for. Once we approach situations looking for how they can make me or the people I care about better, its way easier to find the answer.

CHAPTER 15
CIRCLE OF
SUPPORT

Everyone needs a circle of support. Even the most independent person is stronger when they have someone to help them up.

In this section, we'll go over:
Current Circle: Real Friends
Spreading Our Circle: Networking
Raising Our Circles: Mentorship

I usually ask myself these questions as my relationships evolve into friendships. You don't need someone to fit into *every* category to consider them a friend, but these questions can help you filter through whether someone is cool to occasionally hang around, or if they genuinely care about you as a person; which reveals whether or not I should put in the effort to keep a close relationship.

4 Questions To Ask About Your Circle

1. Do they challenge me to become a better person?
2. Do they have the hard conversations with me?
3. Do I trust their opinion? If not, why?
4. Are they understanding of my situation & growth?

Do they challenge me to become a better person?

This is the characteristic that I probably value the most. The ability to help me grow as a person...as a mature person. I want to qualify this – no friend should have to bear the responsibility of becoming their homie's life coach. I think the most effective way is for the person to possess characteristics that you admire, but haven't honed for yourself.

When I was in my freshman year of college, I met one of my best friends to this day. Although I get along with most people, chilling with him was effortless. We both came from similar areas of Atlanta, had Caribbean roots, a similar religious background, same musical taste, and connected on a lot of other things. The one characteristic I admired about him that I didn't have at the time was his relentless work-ethic when it came to classwork. He would lay out his study schedule, participate in study groups, and isolate for hours if he needed to read material. I would cram before a test and pray I could retain enough information to finesse my way through.

We were both Economics majors, so we had a lot of overlap in material. As time developed, I started mimicking his study habits and allowing his grind to push me to become more disciplined. I picked up valuable skills I didn't see in my previous friend circle. He was able to challenge me to reflect on my own weak spots and help transform me into a better person just by being in his presence.

Do they have the hard conversations with me?

Have you ever been in a conversation with someone, left to go to the bathroom, then look in the mirror and realize you had something between your teeth the whole time?! I'm lowkey tight when that happens. Why didn't they tell me instead of having me look stupid? I would have preferred for them to say something, even if it felt awkward for 20 seconds. Instead of briefly getting out of their comfort zone to help address the issue, they remained silent and allowed the problem to continue.

Bringing up hard conversations with your friends is a selfless act. It can feel awkward, intimidating, and uncomfortable, but you do it because you want the best for them. I've always wanted my friends to let me know when I'm tripping. Whether it's when I'm having problems with my lady, slacking on my goals, or about to get in an altercation over something trivial. Them taking the time to pull me aside, or give me a phone call to talk about something in my behavior that can be corrected, shows me that they want me to level up as a man.

My cousin told me, "Once I know someone's energy, I don't question their intentions." I've always been able to keep it 100 with him on whether I think he's tripping and vice versa. Since he knows I'm coming from a place of love, and with his best interest in mind, there's never any hard feelings. Avoiding the hard conversations doesn't help anyone in the long run.

Do I value their opinion? If not, why?

This question hits on different levels and is the most revealing for me. In order for me to know whether I really value their opinion, we have to talk about topics that aren't just surface level. I'm not talking discussions on who's the best rapper of all time (Jay Z of course), but topics that are personal. In order to get to a friendship level, there has to be deeper conversation than just sports, money, and who we find attractive. If you aren't comfortable bringing up real life issues with your circle, why is that?

The second layer of this question is differentiating between "value" and "agreement". You don't have to agree with someone in order to value their opinion. Sometimes when situations come up, I know certain friends are more equipped to give perspective than others. Sometimes I know a woman's perspective would be more insightful than one of my boys'. But when I've found myself continuing to question whether I should even consider someone's opinion, it has led to a deeper dive on evaluating the foundation of our friendship.

When I've discovered that I don't trust or value the opinion of someone, I've realized one of the following:

- We don't have the same foundational values.
- I don't think they have my best interest in mind.
- I don't think they're being honest with themselves.

I won't say this disqualifies someone from potentially being in my circle, but it definitely causes me to pause and decide whether the relationship should remain surface-level. I know that different perspectives help people grow, but when it comes to issues of loyalty, integrity, and morals, having people who make you second guess those values isn't good for your growth.

Are they understanding of my situation & growth?

A lot of times, people's circles hit them with, "Man, you switching up." This might be one of the most toxic phrases a friend can say. As a human you're supposed to grow and evolve. I'm not the same person I was at 16, 21 or 25. If I never "switched up", that would be problematic. When you're close with someone, they can end up comparing themself to you without being conscious of it. They start to look at any improvements in your life as them being left behind. It's not malicious, but people can start to take changes that someone else makes as an indictment of their own decisions. They believe that if the person they're friends with stops doing what they used to do together, then their homie thinks higher of himself. They take someone else's development as personal.

When I had these types of people around me, I was being held back from being the best version of myself. I would revert back to old actions that I knew I had outgrown. I didn't think I was better than anyone, but knew what was fun for me back then isn't fun for me now. My values and tastes changed. I found joy in different activities and satisfaction in different places. I evolved into a new person with a different spirit.

As I've grown, new friends have entered my circle and some old friends are now casual acquaintances. Not all of my old friends are going to develop in the same ways that I do, but the ones who stay in the circle are those who are understanding and happy for the growth. They don't take it personal and are comfortable with the changes. When you feel comfortable with those around you, it gives you the freedom to allow yourself to grow.

I used to feel lonely because I couldn't find someone who I felt truly understood me. A friend who connected on every level, had the same interests, was on the same journey, and growing at the same rate.

Then I finally realized that that's not what a true friend has to be. Being a friend is a selfless act. They have your well-being in mind and want to see the best for you, even when it doesn't benefit them. Their personality doesn't have to be identical to yours, but can instead be a compliment. You can have different hobbies, but they won't try to make you feel guilty if you're in your own lane. They accept you the way you are, but still hold you accountable for your actions out of love

Networking

Creating a wider circle is called networking. Networking can be seen as a super uptight word, but it really just means to create sincere relationships so you have more options and opportunities. These options can be more dating prospects or more opportunities for jobs. Networking is about getting your name out there so people know you exist, what sets you apart from the crowd, and why you're a good person to know.

Learning to network can take some practice. To help you create a way to build a network, here's a breakdown of the most effective steps:

Share Your Story
Learn Your Audience
Make The Ask
Follow Up

Share Your Story

Stories offer people diverse ways and tactics to learn lessons or share a message. Whether it's the way comedians capture our attention with a story before they say the punchline, or when we binge our favorite Netflix show because the storyline pulls us in. Once we hear the joke or watch the show, we tell our friends about it because it's easy to remember. It works the same way when you share your story to other people. As opposed to giving a list of facts—our school major, job title, or place of birth—we can deliver our introduction as a story, which is easier to remember.

As a start, work on framing your "why" into a 60 second elevator pitch. Your "why" is why you chose to do what you do. An elevator pitch means to give a quick background of what you currently do, hope to do in the future, and how you are the right person to do that thing. You can mix in your personal mission statement and tell someone how it ties into your future goals. An elevator pitch is just a way to give someone a snapshot of your story to pique their interest.

When you're telling someone about yourself, make sure you ACT it out. In order to have your audience connect to your story, be:

- **Authentic** – Just be yourself. People like to be around real ones, not fakes.
- **Confident** – We're all human. No matter their age, accomplishments, or status, you're equal to them.

- **Transparent** – It's ok to talk about things that aren't just surface level. Open up a little and see how they will start to feel comfortable opening up to you.

Learn Your Audience

Networking is definitely more than just telling people about yourself, it's a way to develop new perspective through relationship building. By taking the time to meet different types of people, putting yourself in different types of environments, and learning about different types of cultures, overtime you'll be able to relate to almost anyone in any situation.

The most natural way of doing this is by being curious. Consider it an opportunity to learn about someone or something you're interested in. For example: if someone is from somewhere you've never been, you can learn more about that place from them. If they're from a different culture, you can learn more. If they like the same show as you, you can learn what specifically draws them to it. If they go to your school, you can learn what their experience has been like.

When we stay genuinely curious about other people's experiences, we not only find out more about them, but how much we have in common.

Make The Ask

Shooters shoot. Closed mouths don't get fed. The squeaky wheel gets the oil. However you want to phrase it - *Ask for what you want.*

After you share your story, learn their story, and find out more about how your paths align, don't be afraid to ask for ways they can help you and offer up ways you can be helpful to them.

Sometimes – it's not our strength that's being tested, but our humility. Everyone needs help to get to their end goal, whether they admit it or not. Being too proud to ask for help, or too scared that we'll get rejected just holds us back from elevating.

If you find others who may be able to help your situation, you might ask:
- If they recommend any resources they used to get better at their craft.
- If they are willing to make introductions to people in their nctwork.
- If they have advice for your future.

- If they know of any opportunities you would be a good fit for based on what you've already told them.

If you're networking with someone who's older and feel like you might not have much to offer, consider this:
- If they have kids younger than you, talking with their kids to provide advice from a younger perspective.
- If they are involved in a non-profit, asking if they ever need volunteers or reposts on social media to spread awareness.

Follow Up

I mentioned earlier that one of my favorite affirmations is "I will not take anything personally."

When it came to people not instantly replying to my emails or texts, I really had to reframe my mind to not take it personally. The reality is, people get busy and we can't expect to be their top priority. The have family, friends, kids, jobs, hobbies, responsibilities, and sometimes just need rest from their phones. Sometimes people just forget. Sometimes people type up a response, get another phone call, then never hit "send" (I know that's happened to me a few times).

The main message: Don't get in your own head if they don't respond, just follow up. Assuming someone doesn't want to talk to you is dangerous. Sometimes you have to give someone the opportunity to tell you "no" instead of assuming that's the answer. If they aren't the right person to connect with, that's fine. But closing the door on yourself prematurely can cause you to miss out. The right opportunity will open itself up if you continue to take the initiative.

I used to have an issue with following up, but still being a little petty in the message. Here are a few ways to send a follow up without sounding salty:
- "Hey! Just wanted to check in…"
- "What's good! Following up to see if you're still interested…"
- "Yo! Wasn't sure if you had a chance to reply to my last message, so just making sure everything is straight."

Mentorship

I had trust issues with older people for a while, especially older dudes who looked like me. People I considered mentors either took advantage of me or weren't the people I thought they were when I first met them. This kept happening because I didn't know what to look for in a mentor. I finally discovered the most important parts of finding a mentor.

Find a mentor who aligns with your values.

There are plenty of people who are successful financially or professionally. People who look like they have it all on the outside, but can't even look at themselves in the mirror. Since you already took the time to find out your values in Part 1, now you can find someone that lines up with them.

Take your time.

It's almost like dating. Everyone tries to put on their best face when you first meet them. At times we can feel like we're lost and want to attach to someone off the cuff. But we have to learn to observe people over time, then decide to rock with them based on how they live, not how they say they live. Consider how well their closest relations go— their significant other, kids, parents, etc.—and if they treat people who they don't have close ties to with respect. Before you commit, date them for a little bit.

They don't have to look like you.

I used to think that for me to be able to connect with someone as a mentor, they would need to look like me. I was wrong. One of my closest mentors was a middle-aged white lady from South Carolina. At first glance, I would have thought we had nothing in common. But after going to lunch with her, I learned about her background, values, and aspirations. She had already succeeded in an industry that wasn't friendly to her and went through difficult times that I could relate with. Eventually, I was able to go to her for advice and felt like she really understood me. If I didn't give her a chance because she didn't look like me, I would have lost out on a huge positive influence I've had in my life.

Free Game
The lips can lie, but the lifestyle tells the story every time.

Reflection Questions

Who are 3 older people who you want to speak with to find out more about what they do in their career, what mistakes they made along their journey, and what values helped get them to where they are now?

_____   _____   _____

Who are 3 people around your age who you want to get to know better?

_____   _____   _____

Is there anyone in your circle who came to mind as a "no" for at least 2 of the questions at the beginning of the chapter? If so, how do you want to move forward?

RESOURCES

FAVORITE BOOKS, PODCASTS, SOCIAL MEDIA PROFILES, AND RESOURCES TO HELP YOU LEVEL UP.

Vision Boards

Vision boards are a bunch of images, photos, or words that you pick out to represent what you want in the future. By creating the board, you're able to look at a clear picture of what you want in the future. You can create it digitally or by hand.

Instructions to create vision board:

1. Make a list of goals that come to mind (You can review the 24 milestones you wrote down in chapter 3).
2. Find pictures of images or words that represent the different goals. You can find them online, in magazines, or screenshots.
3. Print the images/words and arrange them to all fit on a large piece of cardboard or posterboard (I use an 11" by 14" size).
4. Glue or tape the images to the board.
5. Hang up in a place where you can see it every day. Also – feel free to take a picture of your vision board so you can have it on your phone.

Favorite Mindset Books

The Four Agreements: A Practical Guide to Personal Freedom *by Don Miguel*
The Gifts of Imperfection *by Brené Brown*
Born To Win: Find Your Success *by Zig Ziglar*
The Alchemist *by Paulo Coelho*

Favorite Mindset Podcasts

Serendipity - Inky Johnson
On Purpose - Jay Shetty
Listen Up with Jess - Jessica Johnson
The GaryVee Audio Experience – Gary Vaynerchuk

Mental Health Apps

Happify: for Stress & Worry
Headspace: Meditation & Sleep
Moodfit: Fitness for Your Mental Health
Sanvello: Anxiety & Depression
Shine: Calm Anxiety & Stress
Suicide Safe by SAMHSA: A Suicide Prevention App

The following phone numbers are for anyone who needs support or knows someone who is in need of help in a crisis.

Bullying: 1-800-420-1479
Crisis Text Line: Text HOME to 74174
Domestic Violence: 1-800-799-SAFE (7233)
Eating Disorders: 1-630-321-5272
Grief Support: 1-650-321-5272
National Suicide Prevention Hotline: 1-800-273-TALK (8255)
Rape, Abuse & Incest National Network: 1-800-656-4673
Self-Harm / Self-Injury: 1-800-366-8288
Veterans Crisis Line: 1-800-273-8255 or Text: 838255

ACKNOWLDEGEMENTS

This is my first book. I don't take my support system for granted and sincerely appreciate everyone for keeping me lifted during the process.

First and foremost, I want to thank God. Your amazing grace, mercy, patience, and love continues to awe me. Without You none of this would be possible.

In the humblest way possible, I want to thank the old me and the new me. To the old me for having the courage to reevaluate his character and lifestyle. To the new me for having the discipline and obedience to pursue His calling.

To my Mom and Pops, and my sisters, Taylor and Chandler. Through the ups and the downs, I know y'all always loved me the best way you knew how. Thanks for being there when I call and helping me grow into who I am today.

To my brothers, Karey Peterson and Tecori-Elder Scott. Thank you for showing me what true friendship looks like and always being there for me. Blood couldn't make us closer.

To Sascha Enders. Thank you for your encouragement, comfort, and pro-bono editing. Blessed to have you in my life.

To all the mentors, coaches, and teachers who have fed into me in one way or another. Jeremy Anderson, Amy Botkin, Anthony Flynn, Perry Chesney, Jerome Franklin, Kyle King, André Kennebrew – thanks for sacrificing your time to feed into me and all the insights I've gained from you.

To my therapists, Nichola Daley and Jocelyn Williams. Thank you for helping me discover things about myself I wouldn't have seen and being a listening ear when I needed to vent.

Shoutout to Philip Cameron, Lloyd Fair, Carlos Guzman, Daniel Hall, Reyna Jones, Reade Milner, Jules Myrtile, Marvel Myrtile, Pastor John Nixon II, and everyone else I consider a friend who's helped me evolve my personal, business, academic, or spiritual mindset.

To Nabila Lovelace and my friends who read first drafts of this book. Thank you for your willingness to provide concerns, reviews, and helpful input.

To the schools, companies, churches, and parents that have allowed to serve their organizations. Thank you for entrusting me to make a positive impact on the individuals through your platform.

About the Author

Kameron Phillips is a nationally recognized inspirational speaker, Certified Life & Leadership Coach, Youth Mental Health Resource, and Diversity, Equity, & Inclusion Advocate who specializes in developing teens, students, and early career professionals into emerging leaders. After being recruited to play collegiate basketball, graduating with a Bachelors in Economics from Emory University, and excelling in the corporate world, Kam decided to walk away from his career in finance and now uses his gifts in full capacity to serve others. Throughout his life journey, Kam personally battled with mental health challenges, veered on dangerous paths, and conquered many other obstacles. His authenticity, transparency, and relatability has allowed him to genuinely connect with his audience and become a respected resource for youth personal development.

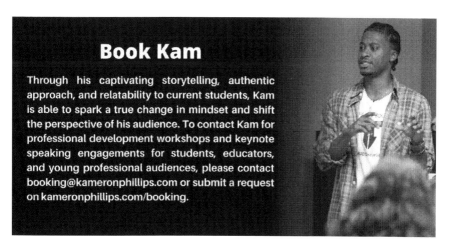

Book Kam

Through his captivating storytelling, authentic approach, and relatability to current students, Kam is able to spark a true change in mindset and shift the perspective of his audience. To contact Kam for professional development workshops and keynote speaking engagements for students, educators, and young professional audiences, please contact booking@kameronphillips.com or submit a request on kameronphillips.com/booking.

Leave A Review

Enjoy the book?

Don't forget to leave a review!

Every review matters, and it matters a *lot!*

Head over to Amazon or wherever you purchased this book to leave an honest review for me.

Much love and many thanks!

Give Us A Follow!

@itskamphillips

www.kameronphillips.com

Made in the USA
Columbia, SC
20 November 2021

49275662R00072